HEAL
FOR
REAL

a guided journal
to forgiving others—
and yourself

SHANNON MORONEY

HEAL FOR REAL

PAGE TWO

Every reasonable effort has been made to contact
the copyright holders for work reproduced in this book.
If I failed to acknowledge your words or ideas, please forgive me.

This book is not intended as a substitute for the medical advice
of physicians. The reader should regularly consult a physician in
matters relating to his/her/their health and particularly with respect
to any symptoms that may require diagnosis or medical attention.
It is always advisable to apprise your physician, therapist or
other mental health professional when you embark on a self-help
journey, or to acquire the support of a mental health
specialist to support your self-help journey.

Cataloguing in publication information is
available from Library and Archives Canada.
ISBN 978-1-77458-099-8 (paperback)

Page Two
pagetwo.com

Edited by Amanda Lewis
Proofread by Alison Strobel
Cover and interior design by Peter Cocking
Printed and bound in Canada by Friesens
Distributed in Canada by Raincoast Books
Distributed in the US and internationally by Macmillan

22 23 24 25 26   5 4 3 2 1

shannonmoroney.com
healforreal.org

To my "sis-tah" Katy

To all those I've had the privilege
of guiding to explore forgiveness

And to you on your journey

CONTENTS

PREFACE

THE REFLECTIONS, INFORMATION and activities in this guided journal are adaptations of the group retreat and workshop program "The 'F' Word" that I developed and led with fellow author, speaker and forgiver (also one of my closest friends), Katy Hutchison. For a decade, we travelled from big-city hotel conferences to tiny, fly-in Arctic communities to help people explore the dynamic concept of forgiveness, and put it into practice in their lives. We never stopped learning as we led.

I'm thrilled to bring our curriculum to you in this format. In this journal, you'll read wisdom and insight from other forgiveness explorers. Through exercises and free writing, I'll guide you to understand and practice forgiveness in your life, in the way that's right for you.

Introduction

WELCOME TO
YOUR JOURNEY

FORGIVENESS IS MY favourite "F" word. I've been writing about it, leading workshops and retreats about it and counselling people about it for over 15 years. I've offered forgiveness and accepted it. Sometimes it's come easily; other times I've struggled. I've even "unforgiven," and then "re-forgiven."

The one thing I know from my journey, and from the journeys of all those I've met and worked with over the years, is that forgiveness doesn't have a singular meaning or follow a linear path. It means something a little different to everyone. Let's figure out what it means for you.

This journal is your place to explore forgiveness—what it is, what it isn't, how to offer it and how to receive it. Ultimately, you'll learn how forgiveness can help you heal from hurts big and small. By the time you complete this journal, you will be able to define forgiveness for yourself—and you'll be on your way to applying it in your life and reaching your goals for inner peace, repaired relationships and freedom from resentment.

You'll be able to heal for real.

Rules of the Road

I LOVE ROAD trips, and as a free spirit, I like to know where and how they'll start, and the general destination, but not many details in between. Some safety rules are good, but other than that, I like to remain open to the process. Here are five road trip rules for using this journal as a map on your forgiveness journey:

1   **YOU'RE IN THE DRIVER'S SEAT.** You can open and close this journal whenever you want—it's yours. You can spend two minutes, two hours or two days at a time. Anything goes. If you make a "wrong" turn, that's okay. Either backtrack or enjoy the detour.

As a warm-up, write about a time when you took an actual or metaphorical detour. What did you learn?

2 THIS IS YOUR JOURNEY. You are entitled to it because you are human. No matter what happened—"big T" trauma or "little t" trauma—and no matter whether you were hurt or you did the hurting, you have the right to explore forgiveness. How about writing yourself a *bon voyage* note? Include some encouraging thoughts and compliments to yourself. For example, "This is hard but you can do it." Or, "It's time."

Dear Self,

_____

_____

_____

_____

_____

_____

_____

Love, Me

3 CHECK IN FREQUENTLY. Someone needs to know where you are and how you're doing. It's always good to have support from a friend or professional in case you need to talk about your process. Who else in your life knows you're healing, or that you're exploring forgiveness? Who might you share your journey with?

_____

_____

_____

_____

_____

_____

_____

I'm here for you too. You can also meet others on the journey in my online community: facebook.com/groups/healforrealcommunity.

4 **PACK LIGHTLY.** You really only *need* this journal and a pen or a pencil. If you can find three photos of yourself, that would be great—one as an infant or toddler, one as a teenager and one current pic. It would be *nice to have*:

- A set of pencil crayons, fine-tip felt markers or coloured ink pens
- Writing paper and envelopes
- Magazines, a glue stick and scissors (in case you like to collage)
- Internet or library access for additional research and resources on forgiveness
- Tea/coffee and snacks

5 **REFUEL BEFORE YOU'RE EMPTY.** The forgiveness process can be both exhilarating and exhausting. Just as it's best not to let your gas gauge dip below a quarter tank (and definitely not wait until the warning light comes on!), it isn't a good idea to push or force yourself to continue journaling without re-charging or re-fuelling. Be sure to take breaks, and follow a good self-care plan (more about that on page 22). It's healthy to push yourself out of your comfort zone, but not out of your safety zone.

And that's it! Ready? Let's get started.

Turn off your devices and find a place of solitude where you feel safe and comfortable. If you are imprisoned in any way, do your best within the limitations you have. Find a safe place in your imagination where you can go. Describe your real or imaginary surroundings below. Use your senses as a guide. What can you see, hear, smell, taste and touch?

_____

_____

_____

_____

_____

_____

_____

_____

While working through this journal, revisit this page or your actual safe space anytime to ground you.

Storytime

I FREQUENTLY VOLUNTEER in my children's school, leading empathy-building circles. Kids of all ages (as well as adults) love to start off by creating an imaginary feast in the middle of the circle. I let them "bring" anything they want, in any amount. I've had the privilege of working all over the world, and learning about favourite foods and why people bring them to the table. I've heard everything from *muktuk* (fermented whale blubber) to apple pie. I have never been in a circle where someone didn't bring pizza.

There is only one rule: Don't yuk someone else's yum. This is how we show respect. If someone *has to* say something about a food they don't like or don't know, they may only say, "Mmmm... interesting!" This approach helps promote open-mindedness, inclusion, emotional safety and the beauty of diversity.

There may be ideas or concepts in this book that don't resonate with you, or that even offend you. You might put forth your own "imperfect" thoughts or feelings. When something feels yucky, I encourage you to keep your journal open and explore where your reaction comes from. Embrace your discomfort as an opportunity to grow your understanding and try on a new perspective.

Food is my second favourite "F" word. We all bring something different to the table. Throughout this journal you will be offered a buffet of thoughts, questions, prompts, stories and ideas. As with any buffet, you can choose whatever you want and how much of it to put on your plate. Some things may be familiar, while others may be an invitation to try a bite of something new.

Just for fun (another great "F" word)—and to warm up to journaling if you're new to it—if you were attending a forgiveness feast, what food would you bring? How is it made, what are the ingredients and why is it important to you?

Imagine you're sitting down at the feast with other forgiveness seekers. Introduce yourself, starting with your name. Which country or culture does your name come from, and what does it mean? If you don't know, make it up!

What story have you been told about how and why you were given your name? Or, what's the story you tell yourself?

_____

_____

_____

_____

_____

_____

_____

_____

_____

_____

Where are you from? Answer this in whatever way feels right.

_____

_____

_____

_____

_____

_____

Where do you live now? Describe in as much detail as you like.

_____

_____

_____

_____

_____

_____

Now let's do a deeper dive. What made you pick up this journal? Or maybe someone gave it to you. Why?

You might not have the answer yet. That's okay! You can just stare at this page. You can also scribble your favourite or least favourite colour all over it, or make a collage that explains what's in your heart and on your mind.

What Is Trauma?

Chances are good that you picked up this journal because something bad happened. Or a bunch of bad things. Maybe recently, maybe a long time ago. Either way, you're finding yourself affected negatively. Let's talk for a minute about bad stuff, and we'll call it "trauma."

Trauma is a distressing event or series of events that interfere with a person's ability to feel safe and in control. Trauma upsets the nervous system and can make it difficult to function in everyday life. In general, there are two types:

"BIG T" TRAUMA

This type of trauma occurs when a person experiences (or causes) a significant, distressing, life-threatening or life-changing event. "Big T" trauma might include:

- Sexual assault and abuse
- Natural disaster
- Car crash
- Death of a loved one, particularly if sudden
- Medical emergency or serious diagnosis
- Job loss
- Enduring, witnessing or perpetrating violence
- Betrayal or breach of trust in a significant relationship

This type of trauma is often overlooked or unrecognized. It occurs when a person experiences (or causes) multiple, smaller distressing events. They may not threaten a person's life, but over time, can seriously interfere with a person's emotional functioning. Picture a woodpecker steadily tapping the same spot on a tree. Eventually, it can bring the whole tree down. "Little t" trauma (or as I call it, "woodpecker trauma") might include:

- Bullying
- Troubled relationships and breakups
- Poverty or money worries
- Addictions (you or someone you love)
- Racism, homophobia, transphobia and other forms of chronic oppression

Both types of trauma can cause the body's sympathetic nervous system to go into overdrive. The sympathetic nervous system (sns) is one of the three divisions of the autonomic nervous system, and its primary function is to stimulate the body's fight-or-flight response. In overdrive, the sns becomes antagonistic to the parasympathetic nervous system (pns), which stimulates the body to "feed and breed" and to then "rest and digest." An sns in overdrive can cause insomnia, intrusive images, nightmares, fear, trust issues, eating and digestive challenges, and hyper-vigilance (scanning one's surroundings for signs of danger). Untreated, this stress can cause long-term health and emotional problems. With support, we can overcome these symptoms and regain trust, health and safety. Forgiveness can help the healing process.

As a trauma therapist trained in EMDR (eye movement desensitization and reprocessing), I work with clients to help us understand their trauma history by making a list of all the bad things that have happened to them, or that they've done. Now that doesn't sound like too much fun, but it is an important step in the healing process— identifying the experiences that have caused emotional, physical, mental and spiritual harm. Even if you don't think they're the cause of your pain now, just list all the bad things that have happened to you (or that you've done). You know, the things that still bother you when you think about them.

The best way to write the list is to imagine yourself as a newspaper journalist. Report the age you were and then the headline of the story. Don't go into the story itself just yet.

Here are some examples:

Age 5, My family was in a car accident and Mum and I were injured

Ages 7–11, Dad started drinking more; I didn't know what to expect when he came home

How do you feel after making this list? Circle all that apply, and add any other feelings you have.

amazed	distressed	sad
angry	hopeful	sick
appreciative	overwhelmed	stressed
brave	relieved	sympathetic
confident	resentful	upset

_____

_____

_____

_____

Ultimately, how do you see yourself at this point? Are you a victim? A survivor? A perpetrator? Maybe all three?

_____

_____

_____

_____

Here's the good news: Forgiveness can help you transform from surviving to *thriving*, and from enduring to *excelling*. Forgiveness has been scientifically proven to help re-regulate the sympathetic nervous system and foster personal development. Have you ever heard of "post-traumatic growth"? It's something in which I strongly believe— it's the positive transformation process that can occur after trauma. Post-traumatic growth is about finding meaning and connection on your healing journey, and a deep sense of purpose in your life. More simply, it's making lemons into lemonade.

Take a moment to picture yourself as someone who has achieved post-traumatic growth. What do you look like? How do you feel? What words or images come to mind? Write them below, or draw/ collage them on the next page.

What Is Self-Care?

Honouring your forgiveness process is an important act of self-care. At the end of each chapter, I'll provide you with a self-care suggestion, or you can do something else that feels right to you. Just promise me you won't let it slide!

"Self-care" is a term we see used a lot in conversations about mental health. Amelia Hutchison is a skilled art therapist on my team at Shannon Moroney & Associates. She is also a trauma survivor, forgiveness explorer and self-care maven. She notes that, oftentimes, discussions about self-care centre on actions that help us relax in the moment. They might be things like getting a pedicure, hitting baseballs at a batting cage or enjoying a piece of pizza. Sometimes these things cost money we don't have. We have to make sure that what soothes us in the moment doesn't stress us in the future.

Activities that feel good in the moment are important practices to have in your mental health toolkit, but what about the bigger life choices that could have a long-lasting impact?

Amelia believes that "self-soothing" is what we do for the present and "self-care" is what we do for the future. Self-care can be less fun or soothing in the moment, but reaps longer-term rewards for our future selves. These are things like looking at your bank account, taking space from family members or friends, moving to a new apartment or booking a much-needed dentist appointment. Both are essential.

Visit Amelia at ameliahutchison.org for more art-based self-care and self-soothing ideas. Know that you don't have to be an "artist" to engage in art therapy. It's about process, not product!

self-care
suggestion

Look at you! Starting is the hardest part and you did it. Before diving into Chapter 1, write yourself a thank-you note and put it in the mail, or ask someone to mail it to you on a future date.

EXPLORING

FORGIVENESS

M Y career began as an experiential educator, and I specialized in alternative and outdoor education at teachers' college. While living in South America, I'd fallen in love with *Pedagogy of the Oppressed* by Brazilian philosopher Paulo Freire. He practiced "popular education"—the belief that teachers should first find out what students already know, instead of assuming they know nothing. I loved showing this high level of respect to my students, rather than imparting an "I know it all" approach. Using popular education philosophy, and drawing from my background in experiential education and our collective training in restorative justice, Katy Hutchison and I developed our first forgiveness workshop for Love Camp, a summer leadership program organized by a revolutionary organization, Leave Out ViolencE (LOVE). Under the white pine trees of Ontario's Muskoka region, we came together with inner-city youth from Canada and the United States to transform experiences of violence into peacemaking work, by exploring forgiveness.

What's Stewing?

TO GATHER THE collective wisdom and knowledge from the group, and to find out what they really wanted to explore, we dragged rustic benches into a circle and put a big cooking pot borrowed from the camp kitchen in the centre. We sat among our participants as equals, not experts, and handed out little squares of paper and a pencil to each person. We invited them to write down their hopes, fears, goals and questions about forgiveness, anonymously. Then all the little notes were put in the pot. One by one, Katy and I took turns reading them aloud. Thoughts, questions and ideas formed a hearty stew that could nourish the growth of forgiveness in ourselves, in each other and in the world. The circle held solidarity and safety.

What's stewing for you right now?

My hope(s) for forgiveness:

_____

_____

_____

_____

_____

_____

My fear(s) about forgiveness:

_____

_____

_____

_____

_____

_____

My goal(s) for forgiveness:

_____

_____

_____

_____

_____

_____

My question(s) about forgiveness:

_____

_____

_____

_____

_____

_____

Here are some things that other forgiveness explorers often have stewing. Circle or underline the ones that resonate with you.

HOPES:
- To find inner peace or to feel "lighter"
- To trust again
- To let go of anger and resentment

FEARS:
- That forgiving someone means saying what they did was okay
- That I'm not worthy of forgiveness
- That if I forgive someone, they will hurt me again

GOALS:
- To forgive myself
- To learn what forgiveness really means
- To move past the pain

QUESTIONS:
- Can I forgive someone who doesn't apologize or express remorse?
- Can I forgive but not forget? Is that okay?
- Can I forgive someone who is dead or who I'll never see again? How?
- What happened affected others too. Am I betraying them if I forgive and they don't?

You see? You are not alone.

What do you think might happen to you and your life if your questions were answered, your fears were assuaged, your hopes were realized and your goals were achieved?

_____

_____

_____

_____

_____

Gratitude

I AM EVER grateful to all the young people at Love Camp for their bravery, vulnerability, honesty and hard work. Some came to our forgiveness workshop summer after summer to deepen their process and to support their peers. One year, a young woman named Miriam Sambe told us that she'd worked on forgiveness for a year, and it had allowed her to have a relationship with her father—something she thought would never happen. Over the years, we saw countless young people repair relationships, end cycles of abuse and flourish with self-confidence, self-love and self-respect. No matter how old you are now, you can achieve all of this too.

Find a photo of yourself as a teenager—or as a little kid, if that feels right—and paste it in the centre of the sun. On the rays of the sun, write words that describe what you will radiate out into the world as you embrace this deep inner work.

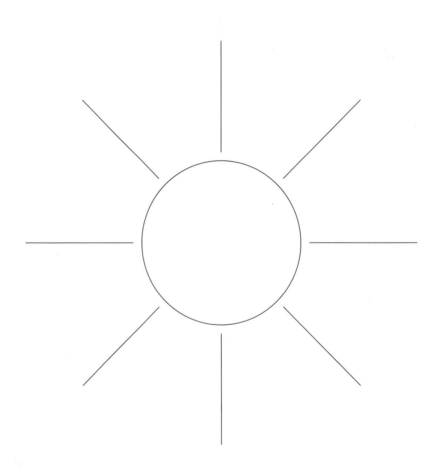

You've started to explore forgiveness: a massive act of self-care. How about taking a break if you haven't already? What do you love to do— that you are in complete control of—that simply makes you feel good? I like to bake cakes. Write a list of 5 to 10 activities below. Take a photo of the list to keep on your phone or tape to your fridge. Commit to doing one small thing each day, and one bigger thing each week.

DEFINING
FORGIVENESS

FORGIVENESS is really strange. This is the title of a fabulous, little-but-big book by Dr. Masi Noor and Marina Cantacuzino, founder of The Forgiveness Project—an international collection of stories by people who have chosen to forgive (including me). Masi and Marina write, "As human beings we are talented thieves. We can rob each other of a loved one, a childhood, a home, a career, dignity, and even an entire future. How strange then that one way of coping with loss is to give something precious to the very person who was caught red-handedly robbing us." That gift is forgiveness.

What Is Forgiveness?

SOMETIMES WE DON'T know what forgiveness is until we experience it, until we offer it or it is offered to us. It is hard to put into words. It connects to many other words and concepts. Circle all the words below that you associate with forgiveness. Cross out the ones you don't like. Add any others that come to mind.

absolution	gift	moving forward
acceptance	growth	pardoning
accountability	happiness	peace
atonement	hard	pity
bravery	healing	possible
compassion	impossible	reconciliation
condoning	journey	religion
empowerment	letting go	strength
excusing	letting someone "off the hook"	transformation
forgetting		weakness
	love	
freedom		wonder
	mercy	

What's coming up for you as you consider all these words?

_____

_____

_____

_____

_____

_____

_____

_____

_____

_____

_____

Here are a few words that come up a lot when we explore forgiveness, and their dictionary definitions. What are your thoughts about these definitions? Try putting them in your own words, and write about a time when you have experienced each one, or would like to.

ACCOUNTABILITY: The state of being liable or answerable; owning up; taking responsibility for one's actions.

_____

_____

_____

_____

ATONEMENT: Satisfaction or reparation for a wrong or injury; amends; agreement following reparation.

_____

_____

_____

_____

COMPASSION: The emotion of caring concern for one who is suffering.

_____

_____

_____

_____

_____

CONTRITION: The state of feeling remorseful and penitent.

_____

_____

_____

_____

_____

EMPATHY: The ability to imagine and understand the thoughts, perspective and emotions of another person and to experience them vicariously or identify with them physiologically (put yourself in their shoes).

PARDON: A release from the penalty of an offence.

PITY: A cause for regret or disappointment; to feel sorry for.

_____

_____

_____

_____

_____

RECONCILIATION: An act of coming together in understanding, as when former enemies agree to an amicable truce; the state of being reconciled, as when someone becomes resigned to something not desired; the process of making consistent or compatible.

_____

_____

_____

_____

_____

RESTITUTION: Reparation made by giving an equivalent or compensation for loss, damage or injury caused; indemnification.

SYMPATHY: Harmony of or agreement in feeling; alignment of feelings with a person going through a difficult time.

Choice

IT'S JUST AS important to define what forgiveness isn't, as what it is. Forgiveness is never about saying that the bad thing or things that happened are okay, or justifying harm. In *The Art of Forgiveness, Loving-kindness, and Peace*, author Jack Kornfield writes, "Forgiveness does not forget, nor does it condone the past. Forgiveness sees wisely. It willingly acknowledges what is unjust, harmful, and wrong. It bravely recognizes the sufferings of the past, and understands the conditions that brought them about. There is a strength to forgiveness. When we forgive we can also say, 'Never again will I allow these things to happen.' We may resolve to never again permit such harm to come to ourselves or another."

Forgiveness might mean renewing a relationship, or saying a permanent goodbye. The choice is yours.

Take a crack at writing your own definition of forgiveness—all that it is, and isn't.

_____

_____

_____

_____

_____

_____

_____

_____

_____

_____

_____

I believe there are three places you can go that will always make you feel better: nature, water and bed. Can you go for a little walk right now? Connect with nature in some way? What about a swim or a bath, or a walk beside a river? Or, can you tuck yourself in for a nap? Rest is powerful medicine.

FRAMING

FORGIVENESS

GETTING hurt is part of being human. Sometimes others hurt us; sometimes we hurt others. The reality is, sometimes the hurt can be fixed, but sometimes it can't and we have to find a way to live with it. Forgiveness can help. It can change the shape of our journeys. It can release anger, fear, alienation, judgment and resentment. It can lower blood pressure, heart rate and even lead to a longer life. It can open the door to peace. Consider forgiveness as a healing gift to yourself, and a radical acceptance of the human condition.

Concepts of Forgiveness

AS YOU CONTINUE to figure out what forgiveness means to you, it can also be helpful to learn about how others conceptualize forgiveness. Here is a collection of ideas and quotations—some by famous writers or leaders, others by workshop and retreat participants I've worked with over the years. A few are mine. I wish I could give proper credit to every brain and heart that came up with them, but I can't, and I hope that's okay. I choose to believe that the authors of these words are the kind of people who simply want them to be shared and don't need the credit. If I am mistaken, I apologize and ask for forgiveness.

Read each quotation as many times as you like. Draw a heart or check mark next to the ones that resonate most with you. Draw an X next to the ones you reject. Draw a question mark next to the ones you're not sure about.

☐ To not forgive is a decision to suffer.

☐ Forgiveness is a continual process, not something we do once or twice.

☐ To forgive does not mean agreeing with the act; it does not mean condoning an outrageous behaviour.

☐ Forgiveness means letting go of all hopes for a better past.

☐ Forgiving others is the first step to forgiving ourselves.

☐ Forgiveness means no longer scratching wounds so they continue to bleed.

- [ ] It becomes easier to forgive when we choose to believe we are no longer victims.

- [ ] Forgiveness means no longer living in the fearful past.

- [ ] Forgiveness is the fragrance the violet sheds on the heel of the one who has crushed it.

- [ ] Forgiveness means freedom from anger and attacking thoughts.

- [ ] It is never too early or too late to forgive.

- [ ] To forgive is to set a prisoner free and discover that the prisoner was you.

- [ ] Forgiveness is not just for the other person—it is for ourselves and the mistakes we have made, and the guilt and shame we still hold on to.

- [ ] Forgive and forget.

- [ ] To pursue the path of healing, we need to remember what we have endured. Without memory there is no healing; without forgiveness there is no future.

- [ ] I never knew how strong I was until I forgave the apology I never received.

- [ ] You can forgive in your own mind and heart, without ever sharing your forgiveness with the person or group that hurt you.

☐ Choosing forgiveness means accepting responsibility for the way you think and feel about being hurt.

☐ Forgiveness is letting go of the right to punish someone, thinking we have the right to punish or feeling pressured to punish.

☐ Refusing to forgive is like drinking poison and expecting the other person to die.

☐ Forgiveness and compassion are not sentimental or weak. They demand strength, courage and integrity.

☐ Choosing forgiveness does not necessarily mean choosing to continue a relationship.

☐ Without forgiveness, we continue to perpetuate the illusion that hate and punishment can heal our pain.

☐ Forgive and remember.

☐ One forgives to the degree one loves.

☐ Forgiveness is the economy of the heart. Forgiveness saves the expense of anger, the cost of hatred, the waste of spirit.

Review these concepts and quotations again and see if you can narrow down the most evocative or provocative to four. Write them out below. Then write the thoughts, ideas, emotions, events and people that each draws to mind.

What might happen if you adopted these concepts of forgiveness into your life?

_____

_____

_____

_____

_____

_____

_____

_____

_____

_____

_____

Storytime

IN OVER 15 years, I've never had a therapy client or retreat participant agree with "forgive and forget," except for the most minor of transgressions. Most people prefer the concept of "forgive and remember." That's for a few reasons. One is simply because it is usually impossible to forget a significant or life-changing harm. Another is that the idea of forgetting seems to dishonour loss or minimize a harmful experience. Finally, there is a sense of fear that if we forget what happened, history could repeat itself—so we stay on guard by holding on to old hurts. Forgiveness helps us to remember without reliving and resenting. We can reframe remembering so it upholds love, respect and learning.

Most cities and communities have memorials—artwork, statues or cenotaphs dedicated to remembering significant events and people, battles won and battles lost. On anniversaries, people gather to pay tribute to whatever or whomever the memorial was built for. Sometimes these memorials become controversial, or downright inappropriate. Take for example the countless memorials built to celebrate colonial leaders. Many are now being dismantled or destroyed, or re-described, in order to honour and apologize to the Indigenous peoples whose land, lives, language and culture were stolen from them. As awareness grows, attitudes can change.

Find your favourite forgiveness concept or quotation, or derive your own perfect definition of forgiveness, and write it below. If you were to design a memorial for your forgiveness journey, what would it look like? Would the words be carved in stone, on a plaque in a garden or sewn onto a banner across the main street of your city or town? Let your imagination run wild. Draw or write your vision.

Visit your local craft shop or dollar store and purchase a wooden frame that you can paint or decorate, and place a printout of your chosen forgiveness phrase inside. Or, find a frame you're not currently using in the house. Place it on your desk, the windowsill above your kitchen sink or anywhere you can see it daily as a reminder or as inspiration. Make your own little memorial—a place where you forgive and remember. Write about your experience after completing this task.

Do you have a junk drawer or messy closet? Why not take an hour or two to clean it and reorganize? It's the perfect metaphor for the process of clearing your heart and mind from the burden of resentment, with more instant gratification! Take before and after pictures to deepen the satisfaction.

UNDERSTANDING

FORGIVENESS

Our families, friends, religions and cultures all give us messages about forgiveness—for better and for worse. Sometimes they are mixed messages. The same bible that teaches "an eye for an eye" also encourages a hurt person to "turn the other cheek." Some justice systems uphold both pardoning and the death penalty.

Sometimes we forgive and it causes controversy or indignation in the people around us. In 2005, shortly after our wedding and while I was away at a counselling conference, my first husband called

9-1-1 to tell police that he had kidnapped and sexually assaulted two women in our community. He was arrested, pled guilty and was declared a Dangerous Offender, which carries the highest sentence in Canada: an "indeterminate period of incarceration"—the rest of his life.

When I chose to forgive him—not what he did, but him, a remorseful human being who had acted inhumanely—I was both revered and rejected. I lost friends and I gained friends.

Your Forgiveness History

BEFORE YOU CAN envision your forgiveness future, it's worth taking time to explore your forgiveness past. This way, you can choose which messages and examples of forgiveness to hold on to, and which ones to let go of. Remember, the choice is always yours.

You may have grown up with one parent who was forgiving and the other, a master grudge-holder. You might have been told that you "should" forgive, or even that you must. What attitudes toward forgiveness were role-modelled for you growing up? Did you see grudge-holding and resentment, love and compassion, or both? How have these examples influenced your attitude toward forgiveness?

_____

_____

_____

_____

_____

_____

_____

_____

With whatever writing implement you're using, circle all those attitudes that you'd like to embrace on your journey and strike through those you don't find helpful. If you have markers or pencil crayons, you can choose a colour you love to circle what you're keeping, and a colour that annoys you to cross out those that you'd like to exclude.

Do you think empathy plays a role in forgiveness? When have you been able to put yourself in another's shoes to see their perspective, or understand the choices they made?

We have all forgiven at times—remember your sibling who borrowed your sweater without asking (and totally stretched it out), or that friend who forgot your birthday? When have you felt the release and peace of forgiveness? Think of all examples, big and small, long ago and more recently. Write names or stories, or draw symbols that represent incidents or relationships.

When has forgiveness come easily to you? Write about this occasion and then doodle around it, or colour in the most healing colour you have in your set of pens or pencil crayons.

What's hard for you to let go of? First think of the smaller stuff—
mistakes, hurts, slights and disappointments from the past. Write
these in your least favourite colour or sharp, capital letters. You can
also shade over your words by pressing hard with your pen or pencil,
or using a yucky-coloured pencil crayon. (And hey—it's okay. You're
human! We all hold on to stuff.)

Now the bigger stuff. What's really weighing you down?

What might it feel like to let some of these things go—to forgive the person or circumstances that caused the pain?

When have you been forgiven, and for what?

Storytime

I'M FORTUNATE TO have many forgiveness role models in my life. It's the most wonderful "work perk" imaginable. Characteristics I see across all of them, from Nelson Mandela to my friend and fellow author Wilma Derksen (who chose a path of forgiveness after the murder of her 12-year-old daughter, Candace), is determination, bravery, compassion and the ultimate choice to let love—not hatred—guide their healing paths. All of these I see in my own mum, Pat, who has never released her loving and kind spirit to the demons of bitterness and resentment. She taught me—by example more than by words—that no one is beyond redemption.

When my siblings and I were small, rather than being punished by exclusion, Mum would send us to our rooms to reflect and write about whatever dispute or transgression had taken place. When we emerged with a paragraph (in full sentences!), then we could meet together with our sibling victim or offender to talk it out. We would agree to make amends, and to do better next time. Holding a grudge was a senseless waste of energy.

With this guidance, I grew up to believe that I am no better than my worst enemy, no less than my greatest friend. I think this has served me well over the years. When we can see the light of hope and the darkness of pain in the ones who hurt us, and the ones we hurt, we can find ourselves on a level playing field. On this ground, we can offer to the "other" what it is that we ourselves need most to heal: understanding, compassion and love. In doing that, we can experience the self-love, respect, strength and humility that are at the heart of forgiveness.

Mum gave a statement at my first husband's sentencing in which she decried his crimes, expressed her pain for his victims and declared that she will always consider him her "son-in-love." I never felt so proud or so supported in my life.

If you're reading this, and you don't have a mum like mine, I share her with you. Her name is Pat.

WHO DO YOU see as a role model when it comes to forgiveness, and why? This can be someone in your life, your faith, in history or someone famous you'd love to meet. What questions would you ask this person?

Trace your hand here. On each finger and your thumb, write a personal characteristic that you love about yourself. Metaphorically shake hands with yourself, and agree to be friends again, or better friends. What would happen if you were your own best friend?

Plan a day to spend with your best friend: you.

ASKING FOR

FORGIVENESS

HUMILITY is a golden gift. It allows us to see that we can be wrong, we can make mistakes and we can hurt others—intentionally or unintentionally. Opening the gift of humility inside ourselves, and sharing it with those we have wronged, is opening the door to spiritual, emotional and psychological growth. When we ask for forgiveness, usually starting with an apology and an offer to make amends, we open the door to peaceful, loving and respectful relationships. Whether or not we are forgiven by others, we can start to dissolve the humiliation that our hurtful actions brought to them and us, and transform it into a more enlightened way of living.

The Art of Apology

I ENJOY *The Far Side* comics. They often convey what I think or feel in a much pithier way than I can. There is one that depicts a couple, with one partner saying to the other, "I don't want your apology, I want you to be sorry." I think it speaks to the fact that apologizing sincerely and meaningfully is an art, and that the words must come deeply from the heart or they are meaningless. We want to know that someone truly has remorse for the way they made us feel, rather than merely for the fact that they were caught. We also want assurance that their behaviour will change.

So how do you know if an apology is sincere? What makes a good apology?

_____

_____

_____

_____

_____

_____

_____

_____

You got it! Sincere apologies do four things:

1   Express regret or remorse
2   Take responsibility
3   Promise to never do it again
4   Seek to make amends (offer restitution)

They sound something like this: "I am sorry for _____. It's my fault, and I promise not to do it again. What can I do to make it right?"

What is the one word that can ruin an apology? That's right: the word "but." What happens to an apology when the word "but" is included?

_____

_____

_____

_____

_____

Have you ever been sincerely apologized to? When, how and by whom?

_____

_____

_____

_____

_____

Did you accept the sincere apology? If so, was it easy or hard? If not, what kept you from accepting it? Is that still the right decision?

How did your relationship with the wrongdoer/mistake-maker change?

Have you ever offered a sincere apology? When, how and to whom?

_____

_____

_____

_____

_____

Was your apology accepted? What happened to you as the wrongdoer/ mistake-maker?

_____

_____

_____

_____

_____

After lashing back at an insulting older neighbour, one of my literary heroines, Anne of Green Gables, was forced to apologize or face a punishment bigger than her crime—she would be sent back to the orphanage. She decided on the former, and thought up the best one she could:

"Oh, Mrs. Lynde, I am so extremely sorry," she said with a quiver in her voice. "I could never express all my sorrow, no, not if I used up a whole dictionary. You must just imagine it. I behaved terribly to you—and I've disgraced the dear friends, Matthew and Marilla, who have let me stay at Green Gables although I'm not a boy. I'm a dreadfully wicked and ungrateful girl, and I deserve to be punished and cast out by respectable people forever. It was very wicked of me to fly into a temper because you told me the truth. It *was* the truth; every word you said was true. My hair is red and I'm freckled and skinny and ugly. What I said to you was true, too, but I shouldn't have said it. Oh, Mrs. Lynde, please, please, forgive me. If you refuse it will be a lifelong sorrow on a poor little orphan girl, would you? Even if she had a dreadful temper? Oh, I am sure you wouldn't. Please say you forgive me, Mrs. Lynde." Anne clasped her hands together, bowed her head, and waited for the word of judgment.

Have you ever been told to apologize, or had someone be pressured to apologize to you? What did it feel like?

Have you ever been told to forgive, or had someone be pressured to forgive you? What did it feel like?

Storytime

YEARS AGO, I was driving from Toronto to Ottawa when I became engrossed in a phone-in program on CBC Radio. The host announced open lines for anyone who wanted to call in and offer up an apology to someone. The concept was that callers might have the chance to unburden themselves, at least a little bit, and maybe somewhere out in the universe, someone would hear an apology they longed for.

I'll never forget the first caller. Her voice indicated she was elderly, and her words were from the heart. "I want to apologize to my best friend in high school. I stole her boyfriend and took him to the graduation formal. I never should have done that—she meant more to me than the boy, and I lost our friendship because of it. It's been over 60 years but I've never quite forgiven myself, and, well, I just wanted to say that. If she's out there, I hope she can hear me. And I hope she'll forgive me."

Her voice crumbled at the end, and it struck me that we all carry burdens—ones inflicted upon us, and ones we've inflicted on others in our own moments of selfishness, hurt, longing and fear.

If you had the chance to call in and anonymously ask for forgiveness for something you did, what would you say? Go ahead, pick up the phone...

_____

_____

_____

_____

_____

_____

_____

_____

_____

_____

_____

How does it feel to write that out?

self-care
suggestion

Eat! You've been feeding your soul with this intense forgiveness exploration. What about feeding your body now? Plan a wonderful meal to make for yourself, or to share with someone you love. Take time to plan it out, shop for the ingredients—and be sure to set the table with candles. It doesn't have to be a fancy meal, it just has to be something in which you delight.

OFFERING
FORGIVENESS

BEING a victim stinks. It means that someone (or a group of people, an institution, a system, a policy, a natural disaster) took hold of your life and caused harm. At first, the "V" of victim stands for vulnerable, voiceless and violated. When we feel those things, it is easy for attitudes and emotions like anger, resentment, blame, shame, fear and self-pity to set in. Soon we find that our relationships, decisions and dreams are directed by that victim mentality.

I believe that offering forgiveness—whether in a direct or abstract manner—is one way that we can transform the negative Vs of victimhood into positive Vs: valiant, vocal, validated, vindicated, vibrant and victorious. We don't have a choice about what happened to us, but we do have a choice about how we respond.

Victims and Closure

VIOLENCE, BETRAYAL, CRUELTY, insensitivity and ignorance cause hurt and create questions in our minds. Yet, so often we don't have the opportunity to express how we've been hurt or to ask our questions of the wrongdoer(s). We live in a society that more often encourages us to stonewall people who have harmed us, and to believe that we will be healed when they are punished. We draw hard lines, silence ourselves (or are silenced) and come to believe that there are no acceptable answers to our questions. We put up our fists in anger, or tap "block" on our devices in haste, grasping ahold of resentment and never letting go. We can easily arrive at an impasse, one in which we think that closure will never be possible. The good news is that closure is something we can find in ourselves.

Think of a situation in which you have been hurt (maybe refer to that list you made at the beginning of the journal). What are the questions circling around your mind that you wish you could ask the person, people or system that hurt you?

_____

_____

_____

_____

_____

Here are some questions that people just like you long to ask when they've been hurt:

What happened?
What were you thinking? What was going through your mind?
Have you thought about it since?
How do you feel about it?
How did you think I would feel?
Why did you do it?
Are you sorry?
What exactly are you sorry for?
What's wrong with you? What hurts happened to you that might have encouraged you to hurt me?
How will I know you'll never do it again?

You see, you are not alone. Circle any questions that are also important to you, or write more of your own.

Think about your own situation. Is there a way that you can communicate these questions to the person who wronged you?

_____

_____

_____

_____

What's the best thing that could happen if you actually asked these questions?

_____

_____

_____

_____

_____

What are the risks of asking these questions?

_____

_____

_____

_____

_____

What if you had the chance to ask for an apology? Who do you want to hear your request, and what words would you use to reach them?

_____

_____

_____

_____

_____

What are the ways you can respond to an apology? Are you required to offer forgiveness, and does it have to be immediate?

There are many different ways we can receive apologies—including those that we offer to ourselves. Here are a few phrases you can try. Mix and match them into a sentence or a paragraph. Then read aloud what you wrote—how does it feel?

- Thank you.

- I appreciate your words.

- I need some time to digest/consider/process this.

- I accept your apology.

- I'd like to continue this conversation.

- It sounds like you've really given this some thought.

- I'm not ready to hear this yet.

- This is a good start. Would you be open to hear more about how your actions have affected me?

- I'd like it if we could start over/again.

- I feel...

- I think...

- I hope...

- I forgive you.

- I'm sorry, too.

What if you never get the answers to your questions, or you can't even ask them because that person is dangerous, dead or you just don't ever want to open that door? Is forgiveness still possible? Yes! A heartfelt apology helps pave the road to forgiveness, but you can also forgive without one. Take some time to write down the answers you most want to hear to the questions you wrote, or the ones listed on page 110. You can also try stepping into the shoes of the person who hurt you and imagine what they might say if they were able to reflect, open up and be honest. Write the script below.

What if someone is just not sorry?

How can we forgive someone if they have caused harm and show no sign of remorse, take no accountability and offer no apology? It may seem impossible, but we can't give up on forgiveness.

In her book *How to Forgive and Move On*, Jenny Hare suggests a few things we can do to help break the vengeance and anger that may have bonded us to the person who caused harm:

1 Be thankful that we aren't walking in their shoes and find compassion for their unhappiness and cowardice.

2 Consider that their circumstances, their upbringing and their personal development have played a role in their behaviour. If our own background were similar to the person's background who caused harm, might we find ourselves in their shoes?

3 What if forgiveness isn't our job? What if it is up to God, the Creator or some higher power? Maybe our job is opening our hearts to the idea of forgiveness so that our outrage, hate and even pain will leave us in time.

What are your thoughts about forgiveness when there is no remorse, accountability or "justice"?

_____

_____

_____

Storytime

SOMETIMES PEOPLE DON'T know that they've hurt us. Or, they might know they hurt us, but they don't fully grasp the *impact* of their actions. We might have to educate them first, so they can have the awareness they need to make a proper apology.

Years ago, I co-led a restorative justice process for a teenager charged with criminal harassment, and his peer victim. This is what had happened: The victim was beaten up in the schoolyard by another student. A bystander filmed the fight and gave the footage to a third teenager who wasn't even there—the one that the court gave me to work with. This teen had taken the footage he was given and edited it to slow motion, put it to music, added subtitles that were derogatory to the victim and uploaded the whole thing to YouTube. It got hundreds of views before the victim learned about it and was able to have it taken down. Police charged all of the offenders: the assaulter, the videographer, and my guy—the "editor and uploader." He was outraged to be charged, arguing, "I wasn't even there!" He and his family were also terrified. They were refugees from Colombia. A criminal conviction would send them all back to where they were murder targets of the Revolutionary Armed Forces of Colombia.

Learning this, the victim decided that such a punishment didn't fit the crime, nor would it give him any relief or justice. He agreed to enter a court-sanctioned restorative justice process in which he would first have the chance to tell the accused all about how he had been hurt by his actions and attitudes. For the accused to enter the process, he had to admit that he played a part in something that caused harm, and he did. After several preparation sessions, the two boys were ready to come together—one to share and one to listen. The accused developed empathy for the victim, as well as respect. A heartfelt apology was offered, which the victim accepted. The victim was empowered to ask his peer for meaningful amends, which included a public apology and enrolment in an empathy-building program. In court, the judge placed the accused on probation to give him time to make those amends, and for me to write a report. This time also allowed the victim to consider offering forgiveness in addition to accepting the apology. He did, when he was convinced by his offender's actions—not just his words—that he was indeed sorry and fully understood the impact of what he had done. And that he'd never do such a thing again.

Both boys found healing in the experience, and so did their families and school community. They graduated the following year and went on to university.

What do you really want to say to the person who's hurt you? The one most on your mind right now. Imagine they are completely able to listen without interrupting, denying or minimizing.

Use a thick black marker, or a fine-tip pen—whatever feels right. It's okay to "yell" in this journal. It's okay to blame, to rage, to cry, to beg. It's okay to accuse. No one can get hurt. Just let it all out. We'll come back to it later in this journal to polish it up.

_____

_____

_____

_____

_____

_____

_____

_____

_____

Have you ever done a guided meditation? I adapted this one from self-love guru Louise Hay, and I highly recommend you dive into her treasure chest of guided meditations, daily affirmations and advice for forgiveness and self-love at louisehay.com.

If we were together, I would read the following meditation to you in a calm, clear voice. You would sit in your favourite chair or under your favourite tree, and you would close or lower your eyes while you listen. Then I would ask you what happened.

But alas! I have no idea where you live. So here are three ideas for what you can do instead:

1 Go to my website and download the MP3 of me reading it.

2 Ask someone you love (who has a soothing voice) to read it to you. You can photocopy or take a picture of the meditation and give it to them so they don't accidentally see your private writings.

3 Record yourself reading it on your smartphone or another device, then play it back. You know what? Sometimes you just need to be your own guide.

No matter which way you choose to be guided through this apology and forgiveness visualization, afterwards I want you to write about what happened.

Here we go:

Close your eyes and take a few deep breaths and when you feel relaxed, imagine yourself in a special place. This special place can be anywhere that your imagination takes you, perhaps somewhere in nature or to a place you feel safe.

In the spirit of forgiving others and letting go of resentment, think of someone who has upset, hurt or offended you. This person might be someone you see every day, someone you no longer see or someone who has died. See this person sitting in front of you, at a distance that feels safe and comfortable. If for any reason it is not comfortable for you to invite this person into the special place that you have created with your imagination, envision them behind a wall of glass, in a room across from yours or see them on a screen. Be creative and do what feels comfortable. YOU ARE IN CONTROL.

Look right into this person's eyes, and know that they are listening intently to you. Can you see that this person was once a baby, like you were? Let your eyes drop to the centre of the person's chest. Imagine that your eyes have X-ray glasses on, and you can see right inside their chest, to their heart. What does the heart look like? Is it hardened, frozen or caged?

Picture the heart breaking open and goodness and love pouring out... pink and red rushing. Now this person can really see you and the hurt they caused you! Lift your eyes back up to this person's eyes. See their mouth forming the words, "I'm sorry." Picture them finding the words to say exactly what they are sorry for.

Now try to visualize something good happening to this person— something that would be meaningful to them. See them smiling and happy. Hold the image for a few minutes and then let it fade away.

Now the person is gone, replaced by a mirror. As you notice your reflection, look right into your own eyes. Say something wonderful to yourself... "I love you," "You are beautiful" or "I'm proud of you." Now take a moment to visualize something good happening to you. See yourself smiling and happy. Feel how good this feels. Take a big breath in, hold it for a moment and then slowly let it out.

When you are ready, let the mirror fade away, and open your eyes and come back into the present moment.

What did you see? How did you feel? What are you feeling now?

_____

_____

_____

_____

_____

_____

self-care
suggestion

How about some social media self-care? Unfollow accounts that have a negative impact on your mental health; turn off your notifications and unplug when you need to; mute and restrict accounts that bring you down; follow accounts that bring positive vibes to your day and support your forgiveness journey. I recommend The Forgiveness Project and Self Love Activist. How about downloading a meditation app?

FORGIVING

YOURSELF

W E are human. We make mistakes. As we grow, change and learn, and as we go through challenges like oppression, stigma, shame, heartbreak and trauma, we stumble and fall. These experiences can shake the ground beneath us, and we fumble around trying to find our footing. Often we are far kinder and more forgiving to strangers than we are to ourselves. Why is that? I'm not sure, but I can tell you that in all the years I've facilitated workshops and retreats, and provided individual counselling, I've consistently witnessed people more easily forgive others for major transgressions, but continue to punish themselves interminably for smaller mistakes.

Forgiving Yourself

SELF-FORGIVENESS CAN BE like the encouragement and love we offer to a toddler who is learning to walk. What do we say when she falls down? Do we chastise her, tell her she's a failure, and that she'll never learn? Of course not! What do you say to a toddler? That's right—you reach our arms out and say, "It's okay, you can do it! I'll help you—take my hand."

What if you spoke to yourself the same way you would speak to a toddler? What could happen if you offered yourself the same compassion that you offer to others?

What would happen if you loved yourself—and forgave yourself through that love? Find a photo of yourself as a baby and paste it below. Around it, write words of love and encouragement. How does that feel?

Now this might be a bit harder. Find a *recent* photo of yourself and paste it on this page. All around it, write kind words of love and encouragement. How does that feel?

Now, what would happen if you told this person every single day, "You are worthy." Try it for a month—be accountable to yourself in this journal, or simply print out a calendar page and keep it somewhere you see every day. Give yourself a sticker for every day that you take a moment to encourage and love yourself.

The Buddha said, "You can search throughout the entire universe for someone who is more deserving of your love and affection than you are yourself, and that person is not to be found anywhere. You, yourself, as much as anybody in the entire universe, deserve your love and affection." What do you think about that?

Author Don Miguel Ruiz said, "Forgive yourself. The supreme act of forgiveness is when you can forgive yourself for all the wounds you've created in your own life. Forgiveness is an act of self-love. When you forgive yourself, self-acceptance begins and self-love grows." Why are these concepts important for healing?

Buddhist teacher and author Jack Kornfield says that finding a way to extend forgiveness to ourselves is one of our most essential tasks. If we look honestly at our life, we can see the sorrow and pain that has led to our own wrongdoing. In this we can finally extend forgiveness to ourselves; we can hold the pain we have caused in compassion. Without such mercy, we will live our own life in exile. What have you been merciless to yourself about? Can forgiveness bring you out of exile in your own life?

Psychologist and author Tara Brach says, "Feeling compassion for ourselves in no way releases us from responsibility for our actions. Rather, it releases us from the self-hatred that prevents us from responding to our life with clarity and balance." Where does your self-hatred lie? What might happen if you forgive that part of yourself instead?

Storytime

DURING THE FIRST forgiveness workshop that my "partner in crime prevention" Katy and I led, we got the sense that our participants were longing for the chance to offer up apologies. I told Katy about the CBC call-in program I'd heard, and we decided to re-create it for the group. Lacking any appropriate props for our impromptu role-play, we grabbed two bananas from the camp kitchen to use as phone receivers (cell phones were discouraged at camp). We invited participants to pick up a banana phone and spill their apologies, while one of us acted as the radio host. After apologizing for whatever was on their heart, the caller became the host. Someone else called in to apologize, and, well, by the end of the session, the bananas were mush, and so was everyone in the circle. So much laughter and tears had been shared, and so many burdens lifted as hope and sorrow were put out into the universe on imaginary airwaves. It was immensely powerful.

I've facilitated that activity countless times over the years (after investing in a collection of plastic bananas) and it never ceases to amaze me what regret and remorse people carry around with them, nor how much we all long to be forgiven. I've heard from many people that the apologies they put out in our pretend radio show became the foundation for apologies that they eventually put out in real phone calls, letters and conversations.

Of all the apologies I've had the privilege of hearing, there is one that remains etched on my heart, word for word. The banana phone caller was a young person in the process of transitioning genders. It went like this:

"HELLO?"

"Why hello, and welcome to the Forgiveness Phone-In! Where are you calling from today?"

Pause.

"Well, um, I'm calling from a camp somewhere in the Canadian wilderness."

"And who would you like to apologize to today?"

Long pause.

"I'd like to apologize to my body."

"Oh... yes, please, go ahead. Your body is listening."

"Okay, well, I'm just really, really sorry. Body, I've mistreated you so much over the years. I've criticized you, I've poisoned you, I've starved you, I've overfed you, I've neglected you and I've even cut you. Yet, through it all, you have held my heart and my soul and you've carried all my pain through this life so far. You've done your best to heal, and I haven't always made it easy. From the bottom of my heart, I apologize. I promise to treat you with the respect you deserve."

What apology do you want to offer to yourself? Go ahead, write it down. Say it aloud. Can you say the words, "I forgive you" to yourself?

_____

_____

_____

_____

_____

_____

_____

_____

_____

_____

_____

We hold anxiety, tension, sadness, guilt, shame and resentment in our muscles as much as in our minds. Play or sing one of your favourite songs as loud as you can (without waking up the neighbour's baby) and dance or shake these feelings out! It feels ridiculous at first, but who cares? This is just for you. No one is watching or judging. Trust me, if I can shamelessly jump around my living room to Van Halen, so can you.

COMMUNICATING

FORGIVENESS

W E live in the age of instant messaging, and while it is wonderfully convenient to be able to text a friend to say you're running late, it is too convenient—and too consequential— to have entire conversations, or even relationships, through short and toneless messages. These are often sent and received while we are in the midst of multi-tasking, and so is the other party. Like many people, I've learned the hard way that in our instantaneous world there is too much room for misinterpretation, and not enough time for reflection and thoughtfulness. We all get hurt when our words are misunderstood or we misunderstand others.

Unblocking

IN A TEXTING or emailing war, we can quickly find ourselves going back and forth with increasing anger, or until one party blocks the other. Blocking a contact ensures an end to hurtful mud-slinging, but it can also close an avenue to reconciliation. Let's get old-fashioned about communication, and reclaim the art of letter-writing. I invite you to write to someone whom you want to forgive, or who you want to forgive you. You don't ever have to send the letter—you may find that the process of writing it is healing enough—but if you do, try to send it by "snail mail" instead of email. Slow down the process. Let the recipient open it and respond when they are ready. Breathe deeply and take care of yourself while you wait. Be okay with the time it takes.

Who is coming to mind as you read this? Who do you want to write to? Why?

Write today's date below. The recipient won't have any other way of knowing when you wrote it, and they might receive it days or even weeks later. It might also take you days or weeks to write. Why is today the day that you are starting this? Let your recipient into your process. Grow your own awareness at the same time.

Now write your location, like your city, or maybe where you are—at your desk, curled up in a chair, in a park or at a busy cafe. What's the atmosphere like? All of this will help to set the tone for your letter, as well as ground you in the present moment.

To further ground you, or calm you if you are anxious or distracted, try this exercise: "Five Senses Countdown to Calm." Write down five things you can see, four things you can hear, three things you can touch, two things you can smell and one thing you can taste. Then breathe until you feel zero anxiety. That should provide some relief and help you focus.

Next, choose a salutation for your letter. "Dear" might be a bit of a stretch if you hold animosity for this person—or maybe you're ready to stretch your heart. Whatever you do, make sure you use the recipient's name. Names are important. If you're writing to a system, use the name of the system. Write your options below and then circle the one that feels right.

Ready for content? Now, this is a first draft, which means it can be an absolute mess. First drafts are always just for the author (trust me, I'm an author). Anything can be edited later—anything except a blank page. So go ahead and get started. Take all the time and space you need. If you prefer to write on a computer, do that. You can copy the final draft onto paper in your handwriting.

_____

_____

_____

_____

_____

_____

_____

_____

_____

Well done! You got it out. How did that feel?

Now, with a highlighter or a different coloured pen or pencil crayon, read over your letter and underline the most important facts and feelings you want to express. Cut out anything that seems like filler.

Next, let's do a little editing and rephrasing to make your letter into something that might possibly be received by your recipient in a way that opens them up, rather than puts them on the defensive. Generally, "I statements" are digested better than "you statements." Here's what I mean:

"I feel voiceless" instead of "You never listen to me"

"When you did X I felt Y" rather than "You hurt me"

Does that make sense?

Here are a few more ways to adjust "you statements" to ensure that you haven't accidentally jumped to conclusions:

"It seems like..."

"I don't understand..."

"I wonder..."

"I feel..."

"I wish..."

Try writing some more "I statements" below.

Asking questions: What is it that you really want to know, or that you just really want that person or system that hurt you to think about? You might want to go back to what you wrote in Chapter 6.

Ultimately, what are you asking for with this letter? Or, what are you offering?

To open a door?
To close a door?
To let go of resentment?
To achieve understanding?
To give or receive forgiveness?
How might you end your letter in a way that clearly expresses your hopes?

It's time to put it all together into a second draft. Take a big breath before you begin. Why are you writing this letter? What is your intent? These might be the very same things that you just wrote down for how you'd like to end the letter—and that's perfect.

Date
Location
Dear _____,
I'm writing you because...

_____

_____

_____

_____

_____

Now, what to do with the letter?

Send it   Burn it   Save it   Frame it   Share it   Other

A "Pro-Con" list may help you decide. It's also always a good idea to have someone else read your letter to provide objective feedback and their outside perspective. Write your "Pro-Con" list below for what you'd like to do with the letter.

PRO	CON

Any lingering thoughts?

self-care
suggestion

You've done so much writing. How about taking a break to read? There is a great list of forgiveness-related books at the end of this journal. Or maybe some fun fiction is the best choice for you right now. Did you know that reading reduces stress, improves writing skills, fosters better sleep, improves attention span, keeps the brain healthy and strong, increases creativity, improves vocabulary and makes us more empathetic?

UNFORGIVING

s it okay to never forgive? Or is an unforgiver doomed to a short life of bitterness and pain? What if you want to take your forgiveness back? Does that mean you're a horrible person? Most people on forgiveness journeys find themselves on a non-linear path. The journey requires patience and practice, not perfection.

Dark Days

WE HIT BUMPS in the road. We have bad days. If we are forgiving someone who died, or someone who killed a loved one, it doesn't bring that person back to life. If we are forgiving a parent who abused us, it doesn't mean we get a do-over of our childhood. If we are forgiving a nasty divorce situation, it probably doesn't mean remarrying our ex-spouse. As we try our best to make sense of the senseless, we continue to grieve our losses. Some days, the grief is more acute than others. Anger surges just when we thought it had gone on a permanent vacation. We might question or even regret the forgiveness in which we once found relief.

Have you ever thought you'd forgiven and then had anger or sadness re-emerge?

_____

_____

_____

_____

_____

_____

_____

_____

_____

_____

How about forgiving yourself *right now* for not being a "perfect" driver on the forgiveness road. How about saying, "Hey, Self—you're human. I love you. It's okay."

Is there someone or something you have decided to never forgive? Why?

_____

_____

_____

_____

_____

_____

Has any of the work you've done so far in this journal changed your perspective?

_____

_____

_____

_____

_____

What is the greatest obstacle to forgiveness that you face?

_____

_____

_____

_____

_____

_____

What could remove this obstacle?

_____

_____

_____

_____

_____

What about forgiveness scares you?

What about unforgiveness scares you?

Storytime

I RECALL A terrible time after my twins were born when I regretted having forgiven. Utterly drained, exhausted and feeling like an epic failure as a mother, I found myself in a rage toward my exhusband—the kind I hadn't felt since forgiving him several years before. "If you hadn't done what you did—if I didn't have to have PTSD and use every reserve I have just to survive and rebuild life—I would be loving motherhood! I would be a great mother! I would have been a mother years ago—young and vibrant and untraumatized. This is ALL YOUR FAULT!"

These thoughts circled hotly in my mind and throat, robbing me of what little energy I had to enjoy my newborns—or even just the ability to sleep a little. I had to release my anger; I had to push the blame, so decided to write my ex-husband a letter. I believe my closing line was, "I unforgive you."

And then yes, friend, I sent it. The unedited, first draft.

Wow.

I felt better for about three minutes, which I think is roughly the shelf life of red-hot resentment sauce, and then I was consumed by my own misery again. The misery of blame, anger, resentment. The exhaustion of regret. The emptiness of unforgiveness.

A couple of weeks later, my phone rang and the caller ID read, "Government of Canada." This meant it was either revenue services or a prison inmate, and since I always pay my taxes, I knew it was the latter. My ex-husband, from the penitentiary where he will live for the rest of his life.

He told me he'd received my letter and that moments later, his institution was put into a lockdown that lasted for five days. He'd sat re-reading my words, and re-living his shameful violence and all its consequences for close to a week. He was calling to apologize again, for everything. It was all he could do, from prison. I was the one with the choice—to accept or reject his apology. To stay in victim mode or break free from it again by re-forgiving.

My phone in one hand, my other hand holding a soother in one baby's mouth and my foot rocking the other baby's bouncy chair, I chose re-forgiveness as quickly as I could. All of us deserved my positive energy. I couldn't change what happened in the past, but I could change the moment I was in.

I like to think that my daughters will know me as resilient, not resentful. That they will only know of the trauma I lived through because I tell them about it, or because they read my memoir when they're old enough. I don't want them to know through my attitudes or actions. I don't want to pass my hurt down to them. I'm committed to a legacy of hope and healing, not one of harm.

What will your legacy be?

_____

_____

_____

_____

_____

_____

_____

_____

_____

_____

_____

_____

self-care
suggestion

How about buying yourself a small bunch of flowers (or a big bunch, if you can afford it). All genders enjoy flowers, so just try it. Do this to honour your process, your journey. When you look at them, breathe deeply and know how brave you are. I buy myself flowers on Fridays and I have for years. This ritual closes my week, and I consciously forgive myself for any mistakes I made, celebrate my successes and know that I'm doing my best. What if you did that too? What if Forgiveness Fridays (with flowers) became a ritual in your life?

LIVING

FORGIVENESS

F ORGIVENESS can be controversial. You know that expression, "Misery loves company"? Well, now that you are on a path out of misery and toward the freedom and peace of forgiveness, some of the company you kept while in that negative place might resent you. You've abandoned them! They aren't ready to forgive, or they don't want to. They might even condemn you for forgiving.

"How could you? You're letting them off the hook! You're betraying me." These attitudes hurt both parties. Yet they can create more opportunities for forgiveness. You can continue to break the cycle of anger by applying the same philosophies and practices you learned by working through this journal: love, compassion and respect.

Transformation

IT MIGHT SURPRISE (or comfort) you to know that many people feel a little lost after forgiving. If the negative feelings related to the harm or the enemy no longer exist, or they have been greatly reduced, it's possible to find yourself dealing with the temporary discomfort of wondering, "Who am I now?"

Who are you now that you're not holding on to hate, lusty revenge thoughts, bitterness or toxic blame?

After forgiving, do you find yourself with more time on your hands? Many people do.

"I used to spend four hours a week writing angry emails to my ex, but now that I've forgiven, I find I don't need to."

"What do I do with my time now that I don't follow my offender's legal process?"

These questions create good problems, but they're problems nonetheless. You may have to get to know yourself again, and reset your daily, weekly or annual schedule. Your relationships might need a bit of a tune-up too. Did your anger and bitterness cause any collateral damage to anyone?

Where or toward whom might you direct your energy now that it is released from negativity?

How many times per day or week did you used to think about the incident or person that had hurt you (or the hurt you caused)? What's it like now? What are you doing or thinking instead?

Is this what you want to be doing or thinking? Why or why not?

Do you have a passion project—small or big—that you can throw yourself into now? If not, make a list of things you love doing, people you like spending time with and places you want to visit. Write dates and times for when you can make it all happen.

What changes have you noticed in your physical health by engaging in the forgiveness process?

_____

_____

_____

_____

_____

What changes have you noticed in your mental health by engaging in the forgiveness process?

_____

_____

_____

_____

_____

_____

How do you plan to maintain these positive changes, and what supports will you need to do so?

What self-care suggestions and tools did you find most helpful while working through this journal? When and how will you continue them? Who or what will hold you accountable to self-care?

Storytime

MY FRIEND Bud Welch lost his 23-year old daughter, Julie, in the 1995 Oklahoma City bombing. He wanted to kill the bombers. For almost a year after Julie's death, he was consumed by vengeful thoughts. Unable to deal with the pain of losing her, he self-medicated with alcohol. He visited the bomb site every day, which added to his rage and desire for revenge. On a cold day in January 1996, he decided he had to change his attitude and focus, or he'd end up dead too. After deep contemplation, he concluded that it was the same attitude and focus—rage and revenge—that had killed Julie and 167 other people. He'd learned that Timothy McVeigh and Terry Nichols had acted in vengeance against the US government for what happened in Waco, Texas, two years before. Bud began speaking out against the death penalty, wanting to end the cycle of rage and revenge.

Bud also identified more victims of the bombing—the families of the bombers. He visited Timothy's father and sister so that he could tell them that he didn't blame them, and that he didn't want Tim to die. He identified with them—they too were overcome with grief, and they also carried shame. He realized that they were worse off than him, because while he could find joy in sharing his memories of the wonderful person Julie was, the McVeighs would never be able to do that about Tim.

About a year after that, Bud found it in his heart to forgive Timothy McVeigh, and he experienced the release of his own rage and lust for revenge. Together with other victims' families, he founded a group called Murder Victims' Families for Human Rights, and they petitioned for the end of the death penalty. Nichols, whose trial was later than McVeigh's, was spared but McVeigh wasn't. He was executed in 2001. A study showed that while six months after the bombing, 85% of the victims' families and survivors had supported the death penalty, six years later it had dropped to half. Today, most believe it was a mistake. They didn't feel any better after McVeigh's execution.

I felt better after I met Bud and heard him speak at a conference. He was the first person I'd ever heard acknowledge the pain and shame of the family members of the offender—the pain and shame I was living with at the time. In validating the McVeigh family, and in speaking up for them, I felt he was also validating and speaking up for me. Bud Welch gave me the courage to tell my own story, and I finally felt forgiven—forgiven for crimes I did not commit. Forgiven for the love I still had for the person behind the horror. Forgiven for any mistakes I made as a result of my grief and trauma.

What positive ripple effect could forgiveness have in you, your family, your community and the world?

_____

_____

_____

_____

_____

_____

_____

_____

_____

_____

Arrival

YOU WORKED THROUGH this whole journal. You are amazing! It's time to celebrate and honour your bravery and commitment. At the end of every forgiveness workshop or retreat I lead, I invite participants to write a single word on a rock—a word they want to keep in their hearts and on their minds about their forgiveness journey. Then we engage in a small ceremony. How about doing something like that for yourself? Check out my dear friend and colleague Kate Love's seekingceremony.com for inspiring ideas. Do what feels special to you. You are worthy.

Describe your ceremony below.

ACKNOWLEDGEMENTS

WITH HEARTFELT GRATITUDE, I wish to thank Katy Hutchison for a sisterhood like no other. I thank every person and community that has allowed me to spend time with them exploring forgiveness. I thank my incredible team at Page Two for helping me translate more than a decade of in-person work into a book that you can hold in your hands and work through on your own, but not alone. Every step of the process has been a joy. Jesse, Amanda, Peter, Fiona, Elana, Alison, Lorraine and Meghan—you have healed me, for real. I thank my kindred spirit Claire Tansey for the referral and for countless kilometres of conversation. I thank my assistant, Emma Jackson, for all her help and support.

I thank *Anne of Green Gables* author L.M. Montgomery for a colourful and memorable example of a forced apology, which I have quoted on page 97. I used an open access version of her work, available online at pagebypagebooks.com.

I thank my "forgivers-at-large" for working through this journal in draft form and openly sharing their journeys and thoughtful feedback: Dr. Izzeldin Abuelaish, KC Allan, Rachel Bird, Serena Hickes, Emma Jackson, Charise Jewell, Marina Nemat, Sima Qadeer, Cara Thomson and my mum, Pat Moroney.

I thank Rachael Lessmann for being the first to say, "I forgive you" to Jason, and for enduring friendship. I thank Jill Goodreau for being unbelievably steadfast. I thank my parents, Pete and Pat, for being an ongoing, dynamic example of forgiveness, and for their endless support. I thank my darling daughters, Anna and Phoebe, for their boundless and passionate love, and for letting me figure out motherhood and forgiving my many mistakes and blunders. I love you all the time, everywhere.

Continuing the Journey

RESOURCES AND
RECOMMENDED READING

SURROUND YOURSELF WITH literature and stories of forgiveness. The Forgiveness Project has a stunning collection of forgiveness stories from around the world at theforgivenessproject.com. Some are also published in *The Forgiveness Project: Stories for a Vengeful Age*, by Marina Cantacuzino.

Here are some more of my favourites:

MEMOIRS

Breaking Night: A Memoir of Forgiveness, Survival, and My Journey from Homeless to Harvard by Liz Murray

Dead Man Walking: The Eyewitness Account of the Death Penalty That Sparked a National Debate by Sister Helen Prejean

Forgiving the Dead Man Walking: Only One Woman Can Tell the Entire Story by Debbie Morris (with Gregg Lewis)

Have You Seen Candace? by Wilma Derksen

I Shall Not Hate: A Gaza Doctor's Journey by Dr. Izzeldin Abuelaish

The Sunflower: On the Possibilities and Limits of Forgiveness by Simon Wiesenthal

Walking after Midnight: One Woman's Journey through Murder, Justice and Forgiveness by Katy Hutchison

You might like my memoir, too: *Through the Glass* by Shannon Moroney

SELF-HELP/PHILOSOPHY

The Art of Forgiveness, Lovingkindness, and Peace by Jack Kornfield

Embracing the End of Life: Help for Those Who Accompany the Dying by Michelle O'Rourke and Eugene Dufour

Forgiveness Is Really Strange by Masi Noor and Marina Cantacuzino

The Grief Recovery Handbook by John W. James and Russell Friedman

How to Fight by Thich Nhat Hanh

How to Forgive and Move On by Jenny Hare

No Time to Say Goodbye: Surviving the Suicide of a Loved One by Carla Fine

Peace Is Every Step: The Path of Mindfulness in Everyday Life by Thich Nhat Hanh

When Things Fall Apart: Heart Advice for Difficult Times by Pema Chödrön

Why Won't You Apologize? Healing Big Betrayals and Everyday Hurts by Harriet Lerner

You Can Heal Your Life by Louise L. Hay

FOR CHILDREN

The Forgiveness Garden (picture book) by Lauren Thompson

The Giving Tree by Shel Silverstein

Martha Doesn't Say Sorry by Samantha Berger

A Pair of Red Clogs by Masako Matsuno

Zen Shorts by Jon J. Muth

ABOUT THE AUTHOR

SHANNON MORONEY, B.A., B.ED., M.A., R.S.W., is the author of two bestselling memoirs: *Through the Glass* (2011), her own story following the violent crimes of her first husband; and *Out of the Shadows* (2019), the story of human trafficking survivor Timea Nagy. Both are published worldwide.

Shannon is also an internationally recognized advocate of restorative justice, a powerful speaker, one of the "world's 50 most resilient people" (Global Resilience Project), a *New York Times* "Woman in the World" recommended writer, and is featured by the international Forgiveness Project. She travels extensively to lead transformative forgiveness and healing retreats for people and communities overcoming trauma, and to keynote justice and mental health conferences.

Shannon is a registered social worker and trauma therapist specializing in treating survivors of sexual assault and trafficking, as well as family members of sex offenders. She has provided expert testimony in court, consultation on crime bills, and she guides attorneys and journalists to pursue trauma-informed practices. In 2019, Shannon launched a line of empathy-building greeting cards, #FindTheWords, available on etsy.com. Proceeds from these cards go to support her healing programs for survivors, as do donations to her Heal for Real Foundation, founded in 2022. Learn more at healforreal.org.

Shannon lives in Toronto, Canada. She is the founder and clinical director of Shannon Moroney & Associates, Inc., "Supporting your journey to post-traumatic growth." Discover more at shannon moroneyassociates.com and visit Shannon at shannonmoroney.com.

HOW TO BRING
THIS PROCESS TO OTHERS

BULK COPIES: Wonderful offers await you and your group of 10 or more. For details and to order, visit **shannonmoroney.com/shop.**

SPEAKING: I love to connect with audiences big and small, in big and small places—including online! To book: **info@shannonmoroney.com.**

WORKSHOPS AND RETREATS: From a half-day workshop at a conference to a multi-day retreat on-the-land, let me customize a transformative experience for your family, team or group. Email your needs and wants to **info@shannonmoroney.com.**

INDIVIDUAL OR SMALL-GROUP COUNSELLING: Reach out if you'd like support on your healing journey: **shannonmoroneyassociates.com.**

SEND A NOTE OF EMPATHY: My cards for unique and challenging times— including an apology card—are available on Etsy: **etsy.com/ca/shop/ FindtheWordsCards.**

HELP THE HEALING: Interested in supporting the healing process of trauma and trafficking survivors? Consider donating to my Heal for Real Foundation: Empowering Post-Traumatic Growth at **healforreal.org.**

     🅧 @ShannonMoroney 🅛 Shannon Moroney

🅕 @ShannonMoroneyAuthor 🅞 @ShannonMoroneyAuthor

🅞 @FindTheWordsCards